CAN YOU SIMPLY
TRUST?

**Building Blocks
of Stronger Faith**

Books by Marsha Sinetar

> *Joyful in the Silence (The Making of a Casual American Contemplative)*
> *Dreams unto Holiness*
> *Ordinary People as Monks & Mystics, Revised (2nd edition)*
> *Don't Call Me Old, I'm Just Awakening*
> *Sometimes, Enough is Enough*
> *Spiritual Intelligence*
> *The Mentor's Spirit*
> *Holy Work*
> *Reel Power*
> *To Build The Life You Want, Create The Work You Love*
> *Developing a 21st Century Mind*
> *Living Happily Ever After*
> *A Way Without Words*
> *Elegant Choices, Healing Choices*
> *Do What You Love, The Money Will Follow*
> *Ordinary People as Monks & Mystics (1985)*

Gift & Children's Books (Illustrated By the author)

> *Why Can't Grown Ups Believe in Angels?*
> *Self-Esteem is Just An Idea We Have About Ourselves*
> *A Person is Many Wonderful, Strange Things*

Monographs From T h e C e n t e r***

> *Can You Simply Trust? (1ˢᵗ gift edition)*
> *Posture of Heart Series, 1 (Preview)*
> *Posture of Heart, II (The Mary Pattern)*
> *Posture of Heart, III (Practice: Inclining the Ear)*
> *Posture of Heart, IV (Contemplative Study)*
> *Dreams Unto Holiness (Inquiry Series, #1)*

*** Center Monographs, currently out of www.mashasinetar.com

CAN YOU SIMPLY TRUST?

*Building Blocks of
Stronger Faith*

MARSHA SINETAR

"Verily I say unto you, Whosoever shall not receive the kingdom of God as a little child... shall not enter therein."

Mark 10:14–16.

For Patty Murphy and her beautiful family, and for Fr. Bob Pagliari, my long-time, East Coast confidant:

My two, trust-filled pals, each from different faith-walks, invariably invite in-depth dialogue about spiritual issues similar to those in this book.

What a luxury. What a blessing.

M.S., 2022

Table of Contents

PREFACE

*Beware of despairing about yourself: you
are commanded to put your trust in God,
and not in yourself.*
Saint Augustine

This book is about the power of a naïve trust. It is a second, revised edition, an architecture of sorts, about "building blocks" of the stronger faith we might want.

Originally—decades ago—with a surge of thankfulness—I wrote these ideas as a treatise for friends and colleagues. The topic was relevant to my life—then; more so now. I self-published the work to celebrate twenty–five successful years as an "entrepreneurial-educator."

Years before, I'd quit my hard-won, tenured position in educational administration to form a solo, leadership development practice. I'd had no business experience or capital, no mentors or contacts, no real affection for networking.

Focus, ardor, people skills—*these* I had.

On the face of it: resigning made no sense. I just felt obliged to follow an inner prompt, a vision: to serve top management in the corporate world just as eagerly as I'd done for students and their families in the public sector.

Mine was no "dream"—it was, as time revealed, a side of a teacher's vocation. Still, what, way back, I'd experienced as a leap of faith, some called "a high wire act." Despite excitement, I'd felt what later is discussed as "holy fear."

Simple trust led my way, proving once more that the foolish things of this world often confound the wise.[1]

Unbeknownst to me, early readers of that booklet circulated it, informally. Soon strangers wrote requesting copies, which I kept mailing.

Now I must thank all of you who sent me private notes about your own growth in trust— the other side of our coin of faith. Your stories emboldened this new edition which reflects my

---

1. 1 Cor. 1: 27-29 (for a more complete description of these first business exploits, see my autobiography, *Joyful in the Silence (The Making of a Casual American Contemplative)*. 2021, MS Teleios Center. www.marshasinetar.com.

current thoughts. I've been working on these notions, testing aspects of trust and other faith factors in the actualities of daily life.

▓

About Building Blocks

In popular usage, *"trust"* and *"faith"* are synonymous. On closer inspection, we find they are related, but dissimilar, largely interdependent, terms.

Trust is a word of *relationship*, as in having assurance *in* someone, even in an idea or thing. It's possible, and done routinely, to bolster trust.

Faith indicates belief, generally the mind's or soul's rise to ideals, to spiritual creeds and certainties. When, at our ground of being, we are drawn into the upper chambers of thought, prayer, or high consciousness, we can become fully persuaded of God's Word and sayings. Or most anything else. (Here, I deal with the former.)

So, *"faith"* implies *conviction*, while "trust" signifies *confidence in.*

In the flow and enthusiasm of writing, I may use thee two words interchangeably. Here, at least, definitions help clarify.

Essentially, *both* words describe spiritual *forces,* powers of underived (i.e., original, primordial) *Life*. And both words express states of being that can and do design, modify, shape, or manifest everyday reality and experience. These two seem to work together as foundational 'building blocks' in the aforementioned structuring of stronger faith. There are other components which I'll also explore.

It's tedious to belabor that architectural theme. Mostly, I'll drop it here. However, I'm convinced now—from direct experience, and feedback from those in my dialogue sessions—that elements such as learning (i.e., how we learn); attention (i.e., how we use or invest our thought and awareness); prayer and meditation (e.g., whether we worship in a manner that lifts the soul into the Presence of God) either assemble sturdy trust and faith, or erode them.

One essential, covered too briefly, is *"true Substance."* As the cornerstone of our edifice of faith, it deserves a book of its own. The point is that all of these, used wisely, reinforce each other to *positively structure* the type of "faith that moves mountains."[2] This system asks us to keep an eye on the Light we have, not on darkness.

To paraphrase a distant, long-gone friend: When these components, or powers, work together, we are more likely to focus on what's eternally Right, instead of tinkering with what we hope to "put" right.

Long ago, and even now to an extent, I placed a great deal of trust in myself, often tormented by the fears and doubts attendant to that habit.

Since life is a type of classroom, I keep learning that, as St. Augustine wrote, it is best to trust God over and above ourselves. No easy virtue, as perhaps you also have discovered.

૭

---

2. This is a method I've come up with, and used, for myself and of course, in my practice for eons, See: M. Sinetar, *Developing a 21st Century Mind*. Random House. NY.1991.

1.

"Simple" Trust

God is able to make all grace abound toward
you, that you always having all sufficiency in
all things may abound to every good work.
2 Corinthians 9:8

To what extent do we simply trust that "God is able to make all grace abound" toward us? That innocent question has needled me ever since I heard a recent report about huge numbers of children who, today, worry excessively.

Apparently, these tormented youngsters include boys and girls of preschool, elementary, and older age. They're said to experience more intense anxiety than the young of previous generations.

Might these youngsters just lack a "simple trust" in God? And,—be honest, now—at some subtle, feeling, complex level aren't we *all* children at heart?

By "simple" trust I mean an inner state of security—like the very young feel, when resting calmly in their parents' arms, or who experience themselves as safe, snug, sheltered. *That's* what simple trust achieves. Isn't this also a synonym of the strong faith that Abraham displayed?

Since Jesus is the "author and finisher" of our faith, any growth at all in that direction is a blessing.

That's neither "blind" faith nor is it thought-less. Simple trust is a way of being, an unsullied, open-hearted state of consciousness: chaste and childlike—but not "child*ish.*" The latter implies immaturity; the former describes the young in *spirit. No* matter the age, the child*like* live in awe and wonder, friendly to the things of God.

Distrust

The worried children in the said news-report possessed the gamut of adult-type ailments: They were fearful, sleepless, had nightmares, and diverse phobias (particularly, school pho-bias). Novelty distressed them.

Essentially, these tykes were apprehensive, as evidenced by physical *dis*-ease of all sorts: Stomach aches, headaches, and other mysteri-ous, debilitating malaise (for which doctors rarely have solutions).

Don't most of our littlest children *learn* to worry, to feel unsafe, and to fret about their futures by observing us? As we *parents* worry, rage, and under or *over* protect them, don't they pick up cues?

Intuitive Learning

I'll return shortly to this topic of how we adults teach and negatively stain our young.

First, consider your own intuitive sense of things—your "education" and unspoken, watchful intake of information as *you* grew up.

I suspect too many of us learned early how *not* to receive the Kingdom of God "like a little child." Too early were we tainted with unease.

Or, if as babes we felt boundless, as if indeed "all things" actually were abounding toward us, before long that idea was ironed out of us. Human affairs can do that.

■

Simple trust has its components—such as how we learn, use our attention, relate to our fears, or walk out our beliefs, values, and integrity.

Let's explore some of these.

For a child, simple trust seems rich with unquestioning. For adults, usually not so much.

Which may explain why Jesus had to instruct his disciples in prayer, and why throughout the Bible we are urged to study, to show ourselves approved, to pray day and night, to meditate on God's teachings, and pray without ceasing.

For adults, and, these days, even many youngsters, simple trust makes demands, has its structures.

For instance, to grow our trust and faith, it helps to discover how we learn, or in what we have invested our attention.

Throughout, I'll stress a mode of prayer that can take us straight into God's Kingdom, if we are ready for it. In poet-artist William Blake's words,

> *I give you the end of a golden string;*
> *Only wind it into a ball,*
> *It will lead you in at Heaven's gate,*
> *Built in Jerusalem's wall.*[1]

ဢ

---

1. William Blake, *Jerusalem,* "The Complete Poetry & Prose of William Blake", ed. by David V. Erdman, Anchor Books, 1988, p.231

2.

Learned Distrust

Abraham believed God and it was counted
unto him as righteousness.
Romans 4:3

Doesn't silent, constant observation teach us so much? The spontaneous noticing of anything (of which we may not even be fully *aware*), directs our everyday mood and choice.

Psychologists use a term called "learned helplessness" when describing some of us. After experiencing continual situations wherein we have no control, we may decide we can't surmount difficulty and stop trying. Just so with trust and distrust. These are learned.

Isn't direct *experience* how we learned most things as children? We saw, sensed, or scrutinized our elders. For better or worse, we *felt* our way into *their* joys, pains, feelings. Depending on what we concluded from our response to those around us, either we decided to trust or distrust our world.

One thing seems clear, each of us grew up believing in our conclusions—feeling safe or unsafe in our own skins, conditioned by our own perceptions.

That last point makes Abraham's uncompromised faith all the more impressive. At some point, the prophet was the first to decide God was dependable. Thus is he now "the father of our faith."

As with all prophets, Abraham brings us a message from God: A 'childlike' trust (again, not childish) is our path to strong faith. Plainly put: just believe God.[2]

Feeling Safe

In this case, the Divine message is that to the degree we walk with, and trust, God, we can also trust our world. Abraham moves through his various trials with assurance. Appearances didn't phase him. Like us, he was completely flawed, yet simple trust saved him.

---

2. Genesis 12:1

Most of us cannot claim to be like that. Not just today's little children, but we adults are cautious. Indeed, these days, even public service announcements on the radio and TV warn us to "Remain vigilant—stay alert to dangers in your midst." In fact, in our usual and quite wholesome state, we naturally *are* wide awake to conditions in our field of awareness.

So early on, how did we learn to feel safe or to distrust? For the latter, I say mostly by absorbing too well the distress signals from adults surrounding us.

As an infant, do you recall the first mice, snakes, or cockroaches you saw? I'll bet you were only curious, not really afraid or disgusted by these creatures.

I, for one, wasn't repelled until someone nearby shrieked, or whisked me away from the perceived threat. These days I shriek, too.

Sensible Concern

Yes, there's often good reason for that sort of (usually adult) upset: We don't want our children touching vermin, hot stoves, running out willy-nilly into the street, or sticking their fingers into light sockets.

However, sometimes—too frequently—we go overboard with alarm.

Secure in the World

To paraphrase an old saying, all children learn from what they see adults *doing*—not precisely from what they *hear* as preaching, teaching, moralizing. Typically, lectures fall on "deaf ears."

Blessed Instincts

Consider philosopher Eli Siegle's proposal: Tiny infants will gaze out at their surroundings and at those around them so as to understand in what kind of cosmos they're living. The young are ever-aware.

Furthermore, from the moment of birth, to coin Siegel's phrase, each "dear being" continually wonders: "What is this world I've come into, and how can I find meaning in it which will make me a greater dear little being than I am today?"[3]

Siegel also suggested that the greatest instinct and *possibility* of our unconscious is to like the world enough to feel safe in it. That

---

3. Eli Siegle, *Self and World*, Definition Press NY, 1981

means feeling secure and easy within ourselves as we really are—*and* feeling safe and at ease with harmless snakes and bugs, and even the unknown.

After all, as we read in Luke 10:19, aren't some of us the ones who believe we've been given "...power to tread on serpents and scorpions, and have authority over the power of the enemy; and nothing shall by any means hurt us."

How might we amplify such ideas? Or extinguish the fear, doubt, and distrust that rob us of joy? As noted, one way is to *notice* what we notice. What do we ingest—eat—as our food of ideas, values, influence?

We might also ask whether our love is of and for the world, or of and for the Divine. Loyalty to the unseen Good recreates us!

When St. Paul spoke of the renewing of our mind being transformational, does he not describe a learning task?

For me, the task involves that *positive structuring* approach discussed in our Preface. It is a multifaceted, highly individualized and creative layering or building up of desired ideas, ideals, "laws," attitudes and behaviors into our psyche.

The method, about which I've written (and taught to clients and students) asks us to try out—test, research– our way into our solutions.

How do we focus on those states, goals, circumstances that we desire? In a sense, as we'll see, we are learning our way into our best future, our "things hoped for" as Hebrews 11 puts it.

Since, here, the goal is a sturdier faith, we'll need to *live* in that solution, *inventively* move ourselves into the perspective of what we desire—and drop our fixations on what we don't want.

So how might we structure more confidence in *the* One who was never born and never dies?

How about trusting in the enabling Love?

ꞩ

3.

The Enabling Love

*There is no fear in love; but perfect love
casteth out fear: because fear hath torment.*
1 John 4:19

"My son," a friend remarked, "plans a walking trip around Europe before getting a job. He called it his 'gap year'. He'll hitchhike, stay in hostels, work as he can."

"What guts," said his dad, "I'd never have done that. At his age—21—I just went to work. Now, I wish I'd gotten to know myself a little more like he's doing."

Consider how exciting life could be if we weren't afraid of making speeches, or starting new careers, taking a year to do nothing, or more fully tackling that which we feel born to do.

Speaking personally, I work at this sort of thing every day.

The grandest gift we can give children is to help them feel safe enough to love life, and themselves, and others. Doesn't that apply to ourselves, no matter our age? Deep down, don't we want that comfort, that self-assurance and peace?

Imagine how abundantly we might live if we felt bold enough to greet our own life as a privileged exploration—mostly of the inner landscape. And as a growth in love, learning, compassion.

Picture how an adult's advance in *emotional* security might help children grow toward their own sense of safety.

Experience teaches me that the agape (or spiritual) love shelters me as nothing else can. It's a feature of simple trust. The more that Love infuses my psyche, the safer I feel. These days my task is to stay connected. We'll return to that shortly.

Self-protection

Haven't most of us built walls to protect ourselves from all possible danger? Or found strategies to ward off the disapproval of others? We either do what our significant others want (parents, spouse, offspring, friends) or rebel against that with a near-adolescent reaction.

Don't we hide from our fearsome (usually imaginary) Goliaths? That's one kind of torment, as Scripture calls it.

Costly Walls

It takes a huge amount of energy to live with such largely invisible barriers. We, when anguished, generally obstruct our own life-adventure with subjective clutter.

No wonder so many young students become upset and "triggered" so easily. They've heard our stories of victimization, our endless cautionary tales. Daily, they watch us become overwhelmed by the stress of ordinary life. How human, how completely natural, to feel this way. Is this healthy?

Ideas as "Triggers"

Listening to news reporters discuss such issues, I've wondered if our 21st Century fears are worse than those of decades past. Maybe we're only technologically better able to find facts, images, and possibilities of things about which to worry.

It's doubtful that we moderns actually *experience* more pressure than we would have one hundred years ago.

Yes, rapid social change and the need to adapt to novelty make life *seem* insecure. The lack of stability for families can take us far from the familiar. Yet mere ideas—concepts—enhance the mind, broaden, deepen our very humanity.

True, constant novelty can heighten feelings of loss and a sense of alienation. Yet consider that a century ago the average adult passed away at around age 30. Today's average lifespan has more than doubled, worldwide. Something must be better.

Improved sanitation, clean food and water, medical advances enhance collective health. That said, could our anxieties be caused mainly by emotional deficits? I say we, and our children, may need to tackle worry as an *inside* job.

Love's "Voice"

Think of today's "latchkey kids" who return home from school to empty houses.

Perhaps they feel alone and forgotten. They don't spontaneously realize that their parents work night and day out of love, care, loyalty for their children. Conversations about that care and loyalty could be needed, reinforced softly, not overdone. That's how stable families structure or address a child's safety needs; they give gentle reassurances, spoken and active reminders of constancy, affection, and the family's enduring values.

How different things might be if we had learned to simply trust Psalm 81's lines, that God has lifted the weight of crushing worry from our shoulders. Now I ask myself: How might I take just a few moments today to rest in that truth?

Each Era's Worries

People say that our era is tough on the nerves. Yet imagine again pioneering life.

Picture journeying cross-country by covered wagon, without a moving van to cart your stuff from here to there. You'd have trudged along behind horse-drawn wagons, inhaling dust, and various unmentionables. You'd have suffered the rain, wind, and ice storms, then blisteringly hot summers, and always untold threats.

Today's books and films teach the tale. Pioneers watched friends, relatives, children, spouses fall ill or die along lengthy journeys.

Now *that's* stressful.

Today, we have wars, rumors of wars, pandemics. Each era has woes. With all that, how might we trust our living God?

Since the Divine Love lives in our "holy" fear, it could help to understand what that is.

৵

4.

Holy Fear

*By faith Noah, when warned about
things not yet seen, in holy fear built an
ark to save his family.*
Hebrews 11:7-8

Some choices are more costly than others. These involve not just unknowns, but also life-changing, perhaps life-ending, outcomes. That's true of all risk: You may succeed. You may fail. The adage, "You pays your money and you takes your chances" applies.

Even with strong faith, we can encounter a *"holy fear"*: That which keeps the soul pure, and leaning on God. Holy fear is full of grace and God's will. Even small choices of this sort help build up simple trust.

In one sense, all fear is holy *if* we turn things over to God. I believe that precept includes the carnal variety, when our senses or outer agents try to dictate terms.

Holy fear involves awe and surrender to God even when life is at stake.

As an example, quite recently I learned that in the late 1800s my paternal grandfather traveled alone to America from somewhere in Eastern Europe. (Latvia? Lithuania? Lapland? It was somewhere way north and way cold. I'm not sure). He was 17.

How did he make that trip? Was he one of the countless indentured servants who gave their all to gain their freedom in the Land of the Free? I'm told he ended up in New York, worked like a dog, and prospered.

I confess to feeling proud—bolstered somehow—just hearing that my granddad had such ambition, such daring, such courage. We never met, but—along with my father—he's one of my heroes. His pluck (or desperation) ushered in what must have been the crossroad of his life.

Was his faith in himself? Or, like Noah, did he have an uncompromising spiritual trust? Again, I'll never know. His seemed the most sacrificial— but also prudent— risk: Surely he weighed the consequences of staying put or leaving. I'd wager he felt a holy fear, then decided, "I'd rather die than live like this." So he voyaged toward things foreign, and saved himself and his future family.

What a heritage.

I'll bet you have a similar legacy somewhere in your past.

Ready or Not?

My granddad's story reminds me that, at times, I've not shown sufficient backbone. Yes, I've sailed into more deep seas of uncertainty than some. And avoided others.

If I can't summon up the nerve, I delay. I stall. I ponder, "*What if?*" — even when (from my heart) Isaiah whispers, "Enlarge the place of your tent…strengthen your stakes." [4] Loving safety and comfort as I do, I resist Saint Luke's word:

> *Go out a little from the land…Launch out deeper and let down your nets for a better catch.* [5]

I plead to God, "Not yet. I'm ill-equipped. Help me. I'm scared."

And then I wait some more. Sooner or later, I sense an inner prompt with an answer. I'd call it 'watchful waiting.' Is that an excuse?

---

4. Isaiah 54:2
5. Luke 5:3-4

The Waiting Game

Is that watchfulness just "waiting on the Lord"? Or mere procrastination? Or, as detailed later, is the soul just not ready for what author Evelyn Underhill called the *inward Odyssey?* Since there are stages and phases to that journey, life's full of delays.

When we fear, doubt, or misconstrue an idea or situation; when we feel, "I just don't know what this means," about something that we hear, read, perhaps dream, it may mean we're not *ready* to understand.

Or, we grasp the weight of what we're considering, and aren't ready to accept the consequences.

Employees who "don't hear" a negative performance review, or who misinterpret what's said are often protecting themselves from bad news.

Waiting to be strengthened, waiting for God's inner prod, could be one way to implement our best choices. The psalms, for example, are full of verses about waiting on God.

Nevertheless, many of us worriers—children included—routinely sidestep the thrill of Life's adventure. As one who, at times, procrastinates shamefully, I appreciate William Blake's idea. When needing a good swift kick in the backside to get going, these lines help me:

> *He who desires but acts not breeds pestilence.*[6]

Sometimes waiting is resistance; sometimes it's just prudent.

What a puzzlement.

Girls and boys who notice continual anxiety in their elders may reason:

> *Well, if Mom and Dad are scared of losing their jobs, or fear so many things, this world must be unsafe for me. I'm scared, too.*

Then again, they may be highly rational, examining the costs and variables of their choice before acting. Looking both ways for traffic before crossing a street is intelligence at work.

---

6. From: *The Marriage of Heaven and Hell.*

Sensible Concern

Indeed, it's proper to watch over our safety, health, finances, and family. Yet those who love the Spirit of Truth are called to *live* beyond appearances, and use their wings of trust and faith to fly high with the immortals.[7] That inmost call makes a big, obvious difference in how we choose to enter or resist a wilderness of some sacred sort.

I ask myself, "When is fear 'holy' and when is it plain cowardice?" At times, I scold myself, "These delays can't be healthy." Still, if not ready, I wait.

Could the answer rest somewhere in between That which *summons* us to follow the Holy Spirit's prompts, and the voice *daring* us to submit to the world's bondage?

That voice urges us to submit to its dark control. I, for one, need ears that hear, wisely, in the Fourth, or "New Man's", dimension.

To repeat: By "following an inward prompt" I do *not* mean foolhardy, reckless gambles. I mean the sacred risk, as Noah proved by working out God's will.

---

7.   Isaiah 40:31; 1 Cor. 15:53-55

When in doubt, "waiting" prayerfully, also dialogue with a trusted, competent companion or counselor seems wise.[8]

The saints, for example, live robustly and magnificently in the world by trusting God's Light to shine *through* their smallest choices. They seem to surrender their "holy fear" to God with a kind of self-abandonment.

Through prayer and revelation, Saint Therese of Lisieux (The Little Flower) determined she'd need God's help in her most inconsequential choices. Meager acts became her path to heroic virtue, her "Little Way" of getting to Heaven.

Whether we are as ineffectual as infants or "masters of the universe," God is here, now, holding our hand, promising,

> ... *Fear not; I will help thee.*[9]

Simple Trust Delivers the Goods

With God, we have what it takes to handle all things.

---

8.   Mathew 4:19; 8:22
9.   Isaiah 41:10-

For instance, when a wordless inner hum strengthens us, can we not sense our soul "singing" our happiest, boldest tune?

Isn't that invigoration the Holy Spirit nudging us onward into Life? At such times, despite fear, we usually feel *ready* to take on our next challenge.

That glad, strong state is a posture of heart. It may not extinguish normal fear; we could be extra cautious throughout a given season of risk. That's just sensible.

I don't claim this path of holy fear is for everyone. However, anyone can refresh their outlook with a new approach to facts, feelings, choices, problems, prayer.

This approach asks us to turn our mind to God—not to the trouble at hand, and then wait on the Spirit of Truth for guidance. It's worth a bit of discipline.

What a difference a God-centered stance can make. As we'll see, with a controlled focus, either circumstances change, or we do.

჻

5.

"Right" Focus

...for they that are after the flesh do mind the things of the flesh...
Romans 8:5-8

When I worried about anything, a late spiritual friend, Norman H., used to repeat, "Love is with you, Love is all around you—*now."*

His reminder turned thought to the Solution. Thereby, instantly, that idea lifted a seeming yoke from my shoulders.

When visiting a much loved family member in the hospital, as he lay dying, and unconscious, I whispered in his ear:

Love is with you, Love is all around you—now.

I'd swear he smiled.

The time to greet the world confidently is precisely when we're lost, afraid, anguished. We're not denying our distress, but rather turning it over to trust, faith, and to the One who says,

Fear not—I am with you.

Moreover, we may want to pray for help or guidance in a manner that lets us be heard. For that, it matters less what we say, than that our mind is *with* the enabling Love—not with our dilemma.

An ancient Hasidic tale explains: When a certain rabbi prayed so that his spirit fused with God, he didn't care what he said,

> *...for then he knew all his words took root in Heaven.* [10]

For our purposes of strengthened trust and faith, *right focus*—the single eye—can shape life's effects, or emanations. [11] As noted, managing our attention can pay off richly, both now, and later.

That controlled "eye" offers assurance, possibly an experience of invigoration, and—for me—safety regardless of some difficulty.

As trust and faith are linked, so it seems are right focus and a sense of safety. (Integrity is also involved, as described in our next chapter.)

---

10. Martin Buber, *Tales of the Hasidim.* Schocken Books, New York, 1917. P. 51 (Paraphrased)
11. *See:* Proverbs 4:23

For instance, if distracted or frazzled, don't our feelings of intactness diminish? We can be scattered, or be hard-pressed to concentrate. The reverse is also likely.

If our "eye" is single, the soul grows full of Light; confidence returns. In the Greek, the "single eye" is defined as "*simple* eye," with its opposite (e.g., "multiple" or "dual") meaning "darkness." Consider the principle that "a double-minded man is unstable in al his ways."[12]

The psalmist David (who had reason to be distracted) tells us why he was sure-footed, even on his most slippery, life-threatening slopes:

> *I have walked in my integrity... I have also
> trusted in the Lord, therefore I will not slide.*[13]

Feeling Safe

David teaches us that his sense of security is tied to two factors: integrity, and a righteous focus. For now, note the relationship between his attention and his sense of safety wherein he could not be shaken. Whenever I have that experience, I know God hears me. Come what may, I needn't worry.

---

12. James 1:8
13. Psalm 27

Like most of us, David often *felt* fear. His conduct was flawed. Like Abraham, David sinned against both God and man. Nevertheless, God considered him a friend because, in part, David's heart was in and *with* God.[14]

We find people with that heart everywhere— living under our own roof, next door, stocking shelves at Costco. They, too, are imperfect, yet use the stuff of daily life to do the best they can.

Thus, by degrees, they'll develop a right focus, and be readied for greater virtues, increased feelings of security.

They'll keep their word, be kind, control their impatience, return a cash-rich wallet found near a bank. When it comes to integrity, focus, and sense of security, little things count.

Furthermore, to be "readied" for making our toughest, holy fear choices, we'll stay alert to our spiritual good.

That, too, requires focus.

Much like the parable of the five wise virgins, In Mathew 25, we need to keep our oil, or source

---

14. As we read in the 91st Psalm: If we set our love on God He delivers us, speaks to us, is *with us in trouble.*

of Light, intact. Oil in biblical terms means the anointing Spirit.[15]

That's how, at short notice, the wise ones were ready to meet their Bridegroom. The other five, "foolish ones" slept, lost concentration, lost out.

Right focus as Skill

Small choices build winning habits. We'll pay bills on time, phone a sick neighbor we don't particularly like, hold our temper when customer service reps treat us badly. Such conduct is learned, perhaps when we're young. Perhaps later.

Like lifting weights, we do a bit more of what's difficult as we can—*not* as we can't. It won't do to try to turn stones into bread.[16]

In this uplifted use of thought we are structuring a more spiritual mind— instead of being at the mercy of our carnal instincts. We might even

---

15. Most metaphysical Bible dictionaries, such as by Charles Filmore, also tradtional ones such as W.E. Vines, *Expository Dictionary of New Testament Words*, define this use of "oil" as the anointing of the Holy Spirit that keeps one ready to meet the Lord.
16. Matthew 4:3

transmute this sort of thing into a "secret" tithe as discussed shortly.

Such self-schooling—or training—can start by pondering our habits, resistances, character, slowly upgrading these. First, it's a meditation that moves thought *beyond* distractions into a deep, quiet awareness.

Every true artist, inventor, and saint cultivates the fertile stillness that comes from the disciplined awareness of what one is being and doing *now*.

It's said that dynamic actors carry that silence with them onto the stage.

In the Spirit, their silence speaks to their audience, which may account for these performers' universal appeal.

On the one hand, we won't want to make a false god or idol out of any such method. On the other, unexpected returns flow from the spirit of genuine calm.

Poise Under Pressure

One woman was crushed after her employer's thoughtless criticism of her work.

Her emotions first said, 'Go home. Crawl into bed. Rest up until you feel better.' Then came an inner prompt: "Think again: Where's your faith?"

In answer, she recollected herself, took a deep breath, uttered 'Help me, Lord,' and returned to her routines. Her feelings obediently followed these thoughts. She marveled at how panic subsided.

Soon, calmer, she revisited her manager's office to state her case. She listed all that she'd done to help the firm prosper. As she told me,

> My manager listened quietly, then admitted she'd spoken in haste. She would review her wording about my performance. Wow—what a huge relief. What a huge lesson,—even in my flawed way, the situation, certainly my feelings, improved.
>
> Attention is my new key to success. For good or bad, it can change everything.

We can't always please a manager—or anyone else. However, as was said in our Preface: To increase trust and faith, we'll consider what's eternally Right—not what we want to "put right."

It's not perfection of thought that edits the images that our senses and circumstances present. It's *Truth* in our inward parts, from which we sometimes hide.

Not to worry. As Elvis Presley reputedly said,

> *Truth is like the sun. You can shut it out for a time, but it ain't goin' away.*

આ

6.

The Integrity Factor

I have set the Lord always before me...
I shall not be moved.
Psalm 16:8

My father loomed large with virtue. Since he was busy, I rarely pestered him for advice. Nevertheless, I watched, listened, learned.

If someone made a cruel joke at another's expense, my dad never cracked a smile, never tried to appease. His icy gaze was disapproving. That quality impressed me so much that, over time, I tried to surround myself with friends and associates who were similarly kind, ill-disposed to malice.

My dad, later my former husband, taught me that integrity is stern, at times non-verbal, certainly not trying to "win votes" or curry favor. In our current culture, what with its political polarizations, harsh judgments can follow those who adopt an unpopular position, and we often easily fear upsetting others with our actual opinions.

Integrity may need to wear a tough, thick skin.

Integrity: Defined and Explored

Our last chapter proposed that if our eye remains steadfastly on God, we shall not be shaken. The "unshaken" tend to possess a spirit of reliability, solidity, sureness, *integrity.*

Which I define as…

living out from *Truth in our inward parts.*[17] Integrity, like Love or goodness, is born of God– not our natural impulses.

Among its features, integrity relates to our uniqueness, such as our…

- spiritual fingerprint; how we are called to God, to live and work amongst others, to a life's purpose, to our particularity or distinctiveness;

- pace, tempo, movement of thought and action;

- moral "rightness," conscience, or inborn sense of "this is right and just for me"; "this, I must be and do" and…

---

17. Psalm 51:6

- sensitivity to nuances of right, wrong, beauty, the dictates of our ground of being.

(The latter may or may not include "psychological types," such as introversion, extroversion, cerebral or "feeling" tendencies.)

In ancient times, four basic personality types were believed to govern temperament as a "law" of life.

Simplistically put, these are: *Sanguine* (cheerful, agreeable), *Choleric* ("fiery," active), *phlegmatic* (unemotional; calm), *melancholy* (quiet, tranquil despite interior states). [18]

Whether any of that relates to integrity, I leave to you.

No Short Cuts

Modern life loves timesavers: These days, cell phones open and shut doors, windows, appliances. We want instant everything.

By contrast, integrity requires understanding and development in the fire of *use*. It can't be

---

18. britannica.com, *ancient physiology*

copied, forced, rushed. Without it, we lose our "saltiness," depth and *flavor* of purpose, character, relationships.

Without it, who are we?

Saltiness gives people a taste of who we really are and where we stand. Salt preserves things; a bit, added to savory food can make a dish. Too much ruins it. Some of us aren't salty enough; some, ruinous.

Integrity and Faith

In translating desired, but unseen, things, into the seen, we're often urged to trudge cookie-cutter paths to success. This is rarely fulfilling, although it could work.

When it comes to finding a new career, a spouse, helping a child deal with a bully, it doesn't always work to look to our feelings, significant others, or to outer sources for advice. Truth in our inward parts seems a sure and better guide— assuming we've developed integrity.

However, experience tells us that faith is a power, with or without help from that inmost resource.

Two contrasting examples might reveal whether faith requires integrity.

Two Opposing Illustrations

Abraham and Sarah trusted God and His promises. Each believed they'd have a child, despite old age. In their case, trust and faith merged as a "seed" planted in "good soil." Their lives flourished with things hoped for, *eventually.*

A fictional example supports everyday observation: faith alone Is a manifesting force.

In "Mr. Selfridge," a PBS series, a dare-devil entrepreneur scaled astounding financial peaks. Using his (mostly non-biblical) trust and faith, he exceeded everyone's expectations for merchandising success.

Apparently based on a true story, the gifted retailer was genuine, but too much "of the world." He trusted shady business partners, was unfaithful to his wife, unavailable to family and friends, ignored his conscience. And, achieved fame and a vast fortune.

Clearly, Shelfridge's story proves that the creative assets of trust and faith need not be integrous to manifest one's heart's desires.

Strong faith (e.g. in a devious plan; in ourselves, etc.) too often produces what we *don't* want. Perhaps we'll ask, why bother with integrity if faith is enough? Fair question.

We've probably all met some who've exuded integrity—projecting reliability, assurance, solidity—and they've been corrupt. At best, their truths appear disturbed.

The immoral can be fully focused on their aims. They're firm, fearless, believable. I digress, but this seems worth the side-bar.

The deceitful may trust that they'll stick to their guns, keep their word—especially to themselves.

However, for any eternal betterment, a hoodwinker cannot please God. Moreover, if inner security is of interest to us, we'll care about morality. Remember as David the Psalmist discovered, to walk in our integrity is to be "unshaken."

Other benefits could surface if we look to our heroes and heroines of that quality. Hopefully, they are of a truthfulness type that lives both fully and blessedly.

For me, saints model such advantages, even though most such lives are rarely carefree.

A study of saintly exprience reveals illness, martyrdom, sacrifices unknown to most of us. And yet they had joy unspeakable.

Our Models of Integrity

As suggested in *The Mentor's Spirit*, we need not know people personally to sense their integrity.[19]

Even at a distance, some people are reliable teachers of the virtues we'd like to embody.

At least, someone's archetypal *essence*— spirit—can resonate with my spirit. It's as though I'm guided by *God's* character in practical matters, as Psalm 36: 9 reveals:

In Thy Light, we shall see light

Impersonal Mentors as Integrity Guides

In a nutshell, not only saints live full out, joyous lives. God's Light flows from all types of individuals in all walks of life—biblical, and long-gone historical figures; diplomats and celebrities; family, friends; rich and poor.

A colleague and I agreed on how to apply a distant mentor's principles for, say, integrity: first,

---

19. M. Sinetar, *The Mentor's Spirit.* New York: St. Martin's Press. 1998

we *notice* appealing patterns of conduct and character. Then we "sew" together all manner of dissimilar but worthy traits that seem to us evidence of honesty, decency, a kind of nobility.

Finally, we'll realize what qualities we're after. Our aim is to display, not merely understand, Truth in our inward parts.

We can't do that by parroting another or copying their formula for fame and fortune. As we see, integrity aims at much more than that.

In my autobiography, I describe the process as being much like creating a patchwork quilt. For traits and lifetime choices that we'd like to emulate, we observe, then assemble qualities we admire. Usually, our intuition, the "gut feel" or hunch shows the way. That method of observation, learning, intuition, coupled with responsible,well reasoned trial-and-error discovery relates more to *joy* than temporal happiness gained from materialistic outcomes.

Also, stable spiritual growth demands *self-*governance. Which might require input from a trusted other—counselor, clergy—not a distant mentor. I've met too many needy types who are unaware they're intruding on other's time, privacy, patience.

It's essential to respect the framework of our far-off guides. There's a context and protocol involved. One rule is to set and to keep clear boundaries—especially when seeking advice from those we don't know, or with whom we work, and from most all fragile relationships. Admiration is a grand influencer, with an arm's-distance observation enough to inspire profound learning.

Uniqueness and Integrity

An art-student noticed that her college roommate disapproved of her casual, unpredictable schedule. The critical girl kept asking, "Wouldn't you be happier with a fixed routine, more organized study habits?"

The creative girl felt the question was manipulative. She knew she needed the freedom to paint as the spirit moved her.

Their Mary-Martha struggle is well-described in Luke 10:41. Note the flavor of that tug-of-war, wherein one sister urges the other to drop her absorptions.

Note, too, Jesus' correction as he admonishes Martha to go deeper into her spiritual capacities, the true Substance of who she is.

That depth or "best part" of Martha (and of ourselves) is the very *foundation* of Truth in our inward parts. Our "best part," or integrity, asks us to accept and live out from the incredible essence of ourselves. Which includes the living God within, and the particularity of our temperament.

We are, as individuals, unique: Not everyone is summoned to God in precisely the same manner.

There was, for instance, a difference between the tempo and temperament of St. Francis and St. Thomas.

The first Saint, quick and energetic, was called a "live wire." The second, slow and lumbering, was known as "the dumb ox."[20]

All true saints have powers untapped by most of us *because* they grasp the full measure of exactly how they are called to God. One is slow and methodical, perhaps considered a fool by onlookers, teachers, parents. The other is fast in everything. A third, a doubter of anything unproven by touch, smell, the creaturely senses.

---

20. G.K.Chesterton, *St. Thomas Aquinas: the Dumb Ox.* London: Hodder & Stoughton, 1933

The saints have powers unavailable to most of us *because* they honor their God-given distinctiveness. Combined with trust and faith, their integrity blesses us, eternally.

We might be dull as dust, plodding along, while our brother charms birds out of trees.

Those we love most may misunderstand or reject us. Let's bear it, along with what Quaker author Douglas Steer often called the "beams of love." Let's live out from the delicate Truth in our inward parts that liberates us while, somehow, blessing others.

ھ

7

True Substance

... I have set before you life and death,
blessing and cursing: therefore choose life,
that both thou and thy seed may live.
Deuteronomy 30:19

During World War II in Germany, a Jewish
woman stood with a line of prisoners. Slowly,
they marched toward a bus heading for a concentration camp. Guards with rifles and police
dogs stood by, ready to kill anyone who disrupted
the procession.

As the story has it, that woman had been
considering Jesus, greatly moved by his sacrifice, and Life. Now, in dire straits, she reasoned,

> *Well, if it's true that we who believe have*
> *died with him, and are now 'hid with Christ*
> *in God,' then no one can see me. It is not me*
> *who lives, but Christ in me. I'm free from the*
> *material grip.*

So she walked away from the others, unnoticed by guards or dogs. She went back to her

home, where she stayed safely for the rest of the War. [21]

How is that possible? In my view, much like those in Scripture who were healed and saved, that more modern woman had touched, or been touched by, the true Substance.

Here we come to our most mystical "building block" of trust and faith.

Miracles, even minor shifts of facts and feelings, spring from the foundation of true Substance.[22]

Granted, we routinely reject such stories and "miracles," as myth or delusion. Or we seek material explanations for *spiritual* alterations of experience. The twain never meet; our attempt to unite these two is futile; if we choose the insubstantial, we are living in…

the sleep of death. [23]

True Substance, Defined

---

21. John Hargreves, *The Indivisibility of the Infinite.* (no pub. Date, audio) www.mulberrypress.com (Paraphrased.)

22. Psalm 118: 22-23

23. William Blake, *Jerusalem* in "The Complete Works of William Blake", Prose of William Blake", ed. David V. Erdman, Anchor Books, 1988, p. 231.

Common usage of the word "substance" means material stuff—concrete slabs, bagels, the Eiffel Tower.

Theologian, biblical scholar, W.E. Vine's more accurate, numinous definition clarifies:

> *Christ is God's 'material...[His constituent]... the real nature of that to which reference is made, in contrast to the outward manifestation of things.*[24]

As our opening story shows, facts and feelings shift *if* and *as* we *know* the Actuality of Christ in and with us. Choosing Life invites God's Presence into our life so that we "and our seed may live."

We are not intellectualizing about Biblical laws, not pontificating from book smarts. Somehow, we intuit Truth by being raised up at the heart above our carnal, material, cerebral programming.

Which ultimately structures more faith and trust into our being than anything we might do on our own. We may not, in the course of each moment, be aware of such "raising up." Which is Grace.

---

24. W. E. Vines, *Expository of New Testament Words, www.studylight.org*

Furthermore, our encounter with the "head stone of the corner" could start with doubt, skepticism, questioning, deathly bad choices. St Paul's conversion illustrates that point: God brings us to Himself whenever it's time.

Life-Choices Can Alter "Facts"

We don't need miracles to modify facts or feelings. Both are malleable.

One day we'll awake feeling poorly, yet an hour later by means of some productive move—a hot shower, an Egg McMuffin, a walk—we'll feel fine. Even serious upsets will obey our acts and attitudes.

It's said time heals all wounds. We can surmount seemingly unbearable things—especially with the ascent of the soul through prayer, love of others, maybe counseling.

The enabling Love works as it will, through months and years, through one's choices, through love that is with us, all around us.

For my part, I am comforted if, daily, I meditate and pray deeply, contemplatively—with Scripture.[25]

When younger, therapy, eventually spiritual direction, helped me resolve childhood issues of loss and long-standing grief.

These days, as a morning and evening basic, prayer is like breathing: Essential. Provided I set aside enough uninterrupted time, the soul moves as if by desire, beyond words, thought, and images into what seems a Divinely authored peace, *true* Substance. For the latter, a decent degree of stillness helps.

Prayer in the Upper Chamber

A simple childlike trust is hard to come by when anxious. As relates to prayer, if I'm upset, perhaps like you, the cares of the moment engulf me. So, here's what I do:

First, before worship of any sort, I'll wash dishes, stroll around in the yard, organize a kitchen drawer. Ordering anything in the physical, instructs my emotions, allows me to "keep my body under…"[26]

---

25. I've described a method that helps me enter that state of "hidden Manna" (Rev. 2:15-17), see my YouTube Archhive, on prayer and the Monkey Mind.
26. 1 Cor.9:27

Otherwise, throughout a worship session, I'm antsy, itchy, fidget, thinking about lunch.

Some say that repeating positive affirmations helps calm the nerves. Whatever gets one through the night.

Spirit-filled prayer works best for me, and has ever since near infancy.[27]

During hardships, don't most of us slip away from our innocent trust a thousand times? We may try to force an inner calm or upbeat mood, but pretense rarely brings lasting peace.

Although anything positive helps for a time, I wonder if anyone really escapes the world's bondage (or a concentration camp) by repeating happy words.

My bias is uncomplicated: Our contemplative *depths* reveal the living Love within so that we "know beyond knowing." For, at that instant, we are *known.* This is key to the whole issue of true Substance, Christ in us, *is made known to us, as we are known.* Then we know God's "material."

---

27. I've described one favorite method on my YouTube channel: #003, *Calming the Monkey Mind.*

That seems, in part, why Jesus tells us that, despite all our good works in his name, "I never knew you."

To be known by God, all prayer must be *real*, unfeigned, Substantial. In Father Borst's inspiring words, there is *only one real prayer—* contemplative:

> *ALL prayer must be real or have a contemplative quality because vocal prayer may never be just a recitation, and meditative prayer never just an exercise in thinking.*[28]

Yes, as mentioned, I am biased. There you have it.

Questioning Experts

I differ from those who call contemplative prayer "monastic."

Obviously, not just members of a monastery are called to deep, transcendent prayer. For one thing, not all those formally canonized as saints lived in a monastery. Nevertheless, most if not all, one gathers, prayed in that "real" fashion.

---

28. Fr. J. Borst, MHM, *A Method of Contemplative Prayer,* Asian Trading Corp., PO Bx 11039, Bombay=400020. P. 37

For another, I'd wager the majority of lay contemplatives pray profoundly. They are not cloistered, but live and work among us ordinary folks.

Finally, as Thomas Merton pointed out variously, there are "active livers" in every monastery that spoil life for the genuine contemplatives who reside there.

I propose that contemplative prayer makes us yearn to give back to God what we have been so freely given. Ours is an intimate giving, rarely overt, not a virtue-signaling in the sight of family, friends, church. Truly spiritual giving is generally unnoticed by others.[29]

Our Secret Tithe

Only God calls us to real and intense prayer from which we taste the "*hidden manna*"—true Substance. Isn't that the Bread of Heaven?

That spiritual food, as I've heard, is the *Actual* of actualities.[30]

God's touch comes diversely as a childlike trust in prayer welcomes the soul into the Kingdom of Heaven, within.

Once again, I disagree with experts.

---

29.   Matthew 6:1

30.   I believe I read this phrase from either Christian Bonhoeffer or one of his students.

Hidden manna is *not* merely symbolic. Anyone called to some decent level of worship is sustained spiritually (i.e., *fed*) by that concealed nourishment. Which, of course, is *Christ, God's material.*

Just as daily nourishment from regular food is necessary to strengthen us, so too is sacred food.

Those who sense a rare contact with the Lord may need less natural food, so great is his fortifying effect.

Which may explain, why, historically, some saints and laypersons existed for long stretches of time only on the Eucharist (i.e., Communion).

Take the case of a Brazilian laywoman known as "Lola." Reputedly, after a tragic fall in childhood that left her paralyzed, she lost her appetite, then lived for 60 years on the Eucharist alone.[31]

Returning to the "secret tithe," the enabling Love eventually prompts our giving *back* to God a kind of spiritual offering; this, from fulfillments *we* receive in prayer or daily life.

Having been infused with Love, our desire grows to "give back" in an intimate fashion. We're

---

31. CatholicNewsAgency.com. (Can.Staff/November 28, 2020) .

honoring the inexhaustible bond drawing us up "with everlasting kindness."[32]

Spiritual food prompts our best giving, however paltry. In this, we need tell no one.

Concealed Giving

Hidden thanks seem a favored method of many who probably use no special name for it. The concealed giving is done as quietly as prayer itself; may even be worship.

One will wash a floor with care, or welcome a tiresome visitor. Another pays for someone's milk at the market, while, silently, thanking God that extra funds are there to give.

One minister's narrative explains:

> *Manna signifies Christ whom God has given to us as a gift. While we are enjoying Christ as our manna, we must take the best portion and offer it to God.*[33]

---

32. Jeremiah 13:3

33. One reference to this method that I've found is described by Minister Witness Lee, *Living Stream Ministry*, Life Study Bible: Book of Hebrews, Lessons 58-60. Several sermons are on You Tube, some not quite on point.

Such ideas are quickly grasped by some; not by others.[34] Since we are each unique, miraculously made, and, humanly speaking, imperfect, let's trust that full understanding comes as befits our life—if not now, then hereafter.[35]

---

34. John 1:5; John 13:7
35. John 13:7

8

Planting for Spring

...but other [seed] fell into good ground,
and brought forth fruit...
Matthew 13:8

𝔄waiting heart bypass surgery, a neighbor invited her favorite friends to an old-fashioned, classic tea party.

Instead of succumbing to worry, she celebrated the beauty at hand: A table set with her finest bone china and silverware, the group's laughter (and tears), and lively memories. Closeness enveloped their shared enjoyment of strong black tea, petit fours, pretty, bite-sized sandwiches with the crusts cut off.

Another neighbor and confidant, Gordon, underwent chemotherapy for cancer. He lived across the gully in a modest cabin, with redwoods circling his home.

Despite chemo, Gordon chose to redesign his garden. He cleared the back lot by himself, chopped down heavy branches, put in new flower beds all alone. He explained, "I love this land, so,

...next summer I'll plant fragrant herbs and something sweet-smelling—jasmine, maybe. I might not be here, but while I am I'll live full out and beautify this spot for the next guy.

Gordon may have had a premonition that he wouldn't make it. Whatever his state, he sowed everlasting seeds in that very good, forever soil about which we read in the Book of Mathew.

Gordon was a bio-chemist, not a mystic, not very religious. Yet, somehow, he *was living out from*—not simply thinking about—the true Substance. Honestly, I doubt he considered things in such terms. He just lived a decent, brave, and fruitful life.

By contrast, a bright, healthy, beautiful psychologist once told me her divorce nearly undid her.

During her separation, she vacationed in Hawaii. (So far, so good.) While there, lonely, depressed, she spent days in her hotel room watching video-flicks about unrequited love.

And ended up feeling suicidal, wondering how to do herself in. Mercifully, she came home intact.

Strangers, and—again—distant mentors can teach us how to reinforce our best intentions, courage, cheer, and wellbeing.

They'll attend to their *inner* climate, give thanks for whatever they can, meditate on meaningful goals, reflect on good news, hang out with encouraging others, and with those they love. They stay engaged.

How helpful it is, under *all* circumstances, to keep doing what we love, value, respect, enjoy— and "give back" as we can. Or, make things better for 'the other guy" as did Gordon.

Puritan preacher-writer John Bunyan insists we haven't really lived until we've done some good for others for which they can never repay us.

Parents who sacrifice their heart's desires to put children through college, or simply support them wholesomely, fit that bill. "First responders," those in the military, organ donors, the UPS person, too tired to walk another step, but carries a

heavy package down a hill for an elderly customer all fit that bill.

We don't always know how much good we've
done. My heroes of trust speak and do little kind-
nesses that lift others out of worry.

Frequently, we'll do something virtuous
ineptly, bumbling our way through a good deed.
No matter. With generous intent, *we* benefit.

Should *our* hearts feel full and happy from
giving, quite possibly, we'll live longer.

A recent Harvard medical study of over
150,000 women correlates optimism and longev-
ity. Over and above race, ethnicity, and lifestyle,
(e.g., diet, exercise) women who felt hopeful
tended to live long.[36]

I suspect findings would be similar for men.
Trust, the enabling Love, and our other building
blocks of stronger faith necessarily construct
greater optimism in us. Might we say hope is a
life-enhancer, lengthener, quite likely, a life-
skill—as are the building blocks we've discussed?

All these are learnable.

---

36.   Harvard Gazette, *Optimism Lengthens* Life. 2022 Harvard.news.edu

In Sum: Trust-Skills are Life-skills

From my perspective, profound prayer is our first life-skill, reinforcing the others. Trust and faith involve our *inner* life. Outer improvements flow from the eternal, Transcendent realm, mostly (but not only) during worship that is *real:* For instance, consider three fundamental life-skills:

- praying in the Spirit—for me, again: *contemplative* prayer—beyond words or thought, not mere recitation;

- meditating with our chosen method [37]— mulling over Scripture, following the breath, mantra meditation: eventually these disappear in pure awareness of "I Am That I Am."[38] One experience seems enough for a lifetime of transformation. The more we effort, the less pure awareness comes– as creatures, we must get our thoughts and feelings out of the Way.

- making responsible, "life-honoring" choices.

The latter involves understanding our 'holy fears", so that, despite these, we might choose life.

---

37. It's often best to discuss meditation methods with a qualified professional: these subtle, very powerful, tools can be unwise for those with certain medical conditions, issues.

38. Exodus 3:7-9

Situations of "holy fear" aside, *rarely* does that mean diving into the deep waters of our dreads.

Let's never force ourselves to act against our fears, our innate better judgment. Fear, as is said variously, is a red flag that warns, "Pay attention!"[39]

Those I've admired most in that regard continually use a predicament to study the deepest Reality—the way things really are. Which, ultimately, prompts healthy response.

Not everyone can, or wants to, set their mind on God and God's power. Not everyone can, or wants to, attend to what works (rather than stew over "the problem").

Even so, "life-skills" involve learning, growth, the building of wisdom, power and trust in basic capacities that address everyday life. Solving problems, enjoying emotional stability, worthy relationships—these ask for *acquired life*-skills. Some of us develop these at our parents' knee. Some, much later. Some, never.

Thinking out from our solutions, or "things hoped for," acting in small, responsible ways so

---

39. Please see *Afterward*

as to step into those things desired, and speaking from the vantage point of *having received* the things hoped for, these habits seem, to me, learnable.

Consider speech: It may *feel* false to talk of having what we don't have yet. However, there's sheer power in our words. Our voice bears witness to our faith.

How amazing it is that speech *releases* the Holy Spirit passing through our breath![40]

None of this is a paint-by-numbers learning, although some trusted other or course could be a guide. Here's where distant mentors or anyone we don't know well can set a teachable example.

When asked, "how are you?", the clerk at my local market answers cheerfully, "I'm very well, thank you!" He smiles, keeps working, sounds sincere.

One never knows exactly how that man feels, but his words sure do uplift those of us who hear him.

That's the point—*his* speech is a gift to others, while over time, he benefits himself. His life

---

40. 1 Corinthians 2:4-6 "..speech and preaching was…in demonstration of the Holy Spirit."

skills underscore the rule: "He who waters shall be watered."[41]

One woman is a case example of how *sensible trust-filled steps can move one* from an unseen desire to the seen manifestation.

Impoverished in youth, she recalled putting small luxuries, like a high-end lipstick, on lay-away:

> *Just plunking down a few bucks for something I really wanted, speaking my desires and thanks, gave me confidence that I could, and always would take care of myself.*
>
> *It felt like being in a play where I was financially secure. And so, in fact, it came to pass. Life imitates art.*

Using our mind purposefully helps.

Attention As Power

Instead of pushing ourselves into this or that idea or behavior, consider the power of the mind. Thought produces effects whether we're aware of it or not.

---

41. Proverbs 11

While writing these pages, I heard about a young single man preoccupied with fears about the future. He'd pasted images of the Doomsday Clock on his wall, preparing for what he believed was the end of civilization. He joined like-minded survivalists, trusting in death, not life.

His mind shifted back to life when, at one meeting, he met his soul-mate. Suddenly love caught his attention.

I'm told that, today, that same young man is passionately, enthusiastically preoccupied with his new, affection-filled life—*not* with the end of the world. How heartwarming to learn once more of the regenerative efffects of loving, wholesome thought.

■

Anyone chooses life when preparing for a marriage, the birth of a baby, a new home, an herb garden. Even, during a chilling season, we can hone our thinking, choosing, speaking skills by, first, dwelling on beauty, virtue, "whatsoever things are true."[42] Truth in our mind will, ultimately, express itself.

---

42. Philipeans 4: 6-8

We practice growing such skills when we don't *feel* like it—as with any ability. In a sense, our resistance is sometimes the best window of opportunity to plant "good seed in good soil."

Imagine It

Picture what we adults could teach ourselves, each other, and children about the privilege of being alive *if* we made it our job to…

- infuse our corner of the world with a robust expectation of the best future, and

- if necessary, endured all things with Abraham's type of strong faith.

How true the saying, we are a work in progress. When all seems bleak, let's trust God as our consuming fire, to change us and all things, even death, into Himself.[43]

Does this sound like your author has mastered all such tasks? She practices the art, life-skills, and virtues of simple trust *daily*—even while writing these lines.

---

43. Meister Eckhart's treatment of the Deuteronomy verse.

Like the disciples, she prays, "Lord, increase my faith." [44]

Surely, that prayer takes us back to fundamentals. Surely, the practice of elementary things itself, done rightly, retrains us in the first rule of simple trust and greater faith:

Only *one* God brings us out of this world's house of bondage.[45]

Vince Lombardi, the great NFL coach, believed in reviewing the basics. He'd repeat to his championship players (while holding up a pigskin):

"This *is a football.*"

Just so, I pray about these basics of simple trust and stronger faith and hope to be heard.

It's said that the only prayers that God answers are those that *reach* heaven. In which case, mustn't we pray unceasingly, at the accept-

---

44. Luke 17:5
45. Exodus 20:1-3

able time—*now*—with utterances that are real, offered up in the Presence and Spirit of God?

For me, that means being free to say short, homely prayers, in childlike little ways whenever need arises:

Such as this little prayer of mine that, in closing this book, I want to share with you:

My God, my Father, I trust you.[46]

ᔍ

---

46. Scripture's many verses for this sort of prayer include Proverbs 3:5-6; John 14:20.

Afterword
Gentle, Like a Mother

Let's be clear: Simple trust is embedded in the Divine Love.[47] Unless Love's voice and character live at the seat of the soul, distrust always whispers:

> *Surely, God doesn't really expect you to*
> *ignore your natural comfort or understanding,*
> *does He?*

Added to that undertone are feelings of shame about our normal, if mostly irrational, emotions such as anger, greed, jealousy, suspicion, cynicism, skepticism. All this sort of thing is rooted in fear and *learned* helplessness.

We may try to, but cannot, hide, suppress, ignore, psychoanalyze, or war against such passions.

They fester down deep, corrupting our joy, good health, happy friendships. So if we can't tamp down these feelings, or brow-beat ourselves into a more trusting state, what's the solution?

---

47. Eph. 3:17

Only perfect love casts out our dreads. That's because fear is related to punishment. [48]

As noted throughout, we need to (a) love ourselves—just as we love one another, and (b) cultivate a more encouraging posture of heart toward our negative emotions. Naturally, that doesn't mean narcissism's self-love, or *acting out* or dwelling on the negativity we feel. It entails tempering the harsh inner climate we may have adopted toward our fears.

Further, I believe one aspect of *one type* of prayer—*contemplative*—moves the soul toward non-punitive love, the enabling Love.

I am now speaking exclusively about our *feelings* of fear—not about behaviors, situations, or the like.

Admittedly, my outlook on prayer is a bias. However, a long lifetime of direct and intricate experience—personal and professional—in set-tings and with constituents more varied in age, type, and scope than almost anyone you can name—has convinced me: Contemplative prayer (or at least its wordless, reflective movement of awareness) can answer most common ills.

---

48. John 4:18 (KJV; NIV, etc.)

Such prayer is subtle, powerful, and usually best begun *after* consultation with, at minimum, an appropriate, *qualified*, professional with expertise in the field. Here, I include a knowledgeable physician. [49]

Thomas Merton's comment, on some recording or other, that "unreality lives at the heart of every problem" highlights my point.[50] Sooner or later, contemplative prayer lifts our awareness "up", or out of, unreality. Which is shocking for some since that shakes up everything that can be shaken. A closer look at that prayer may explain:

Contemplative prayer emulates a good and wholesome mother's love. Which seems as close to Godly care as anything we find on earth.

That also suggests contemplative prayer(s), *done rightly,* ultimately guide the soul *into* the Reality to which vocal prayer (recitations) and meditation (mental action; thought) can only

---

49. "Common ills" would *not* include extremes of panic, pathologies, mental or physical illnesses such as are best treated by, or at least guided by, a qualified helping professional, physician etc.

50. I heard this years ago, never forgot it, but necessarily paraphrased his remark.

point. I amplify some of the above with three considerations:

1. *"Done rightly"* entails maturity, perhaps spiritual direction, certainly time, discipline, patience, daily practice, and the mental, even physical, health to sustain its subtle, transformative insights.

2. As to "shaking things up": Like inordinate cups of espresso, consumed irresponsibly, contemplative prayer may be too strong for some. Such as those with serious PTSD, blood pressure or heart irregularities and suchlike. (There are those who take a legalistic, inflexible stance toward all this. I am not one. Please see various footnotes.)

3. Re: proper, "right" practice: Such worship is no quick fix. I'd call it part of a specific type of devotional life. It's *daily*, God-centered devotion; not hits of LSD or hallucinogenic tea.

More: For me, the transcendent feature of contemplation has been Wisdom's method of handling fear. Gradually, phantoms of anxiety have loosened their hold, false lessons have faded. My transformations have been progressive, not overnight. The more trust I show forth, the quicker improvement shows up.

It's faster for some—like our saints or even ordinary people who, despite human flaws, seem to fan their flame of desire for union with God more intensely than most.

One thing for sure: Lukewarm won't do.

Father J. Borst, whose ideas continually enhance my life, wrote that contemplative prayer

> *is the only real prayer [in that it takes us straight to] the actuality of God's Presence, and to the healing, cleansing of our soul by the infusion of the Holy Spirit.* [51]

True, I am, by temperament and the life I lead, predisposed to assert such convictions. It's also true that transcendent, Spirit-filled prayer speaks a language alien to our carnal mind and five senses.

In all of this, I'm reminded of the raw affection of the Lord's protective "mother love."

A sheltering care is obvious in Jesus as he tells Jerusalem that he'd often wanted to gather them under his wing, "as a mother hen gathereth her chicks...." [52]

---

51. Fr. J. Borst, *A Method of Contemplative Prayer,* 2nd Ed., R.B. Pinto, Bombay, India. (No pub. Date) itals, mine

52. Luke 13: 34-5

Sadly, many of us are ill-equipped, emotionally and intellectually, for the purity and warmth of such love. We've *learned* to be harsh with ourselves. Further, we may be dominated by false, secular or relational, gods.

What then?

Then, we might need to arm ourselves with capacity enough to carry the agape love. That's the God-kind-of-love born of the Holy Spirit, Whose temple we are.[53] All this is a development of soul-strength, not physical.

So, we help ourselves to follow God's prompts, just as we prepare the very young for reading when they don't even recognize the alphabet. We acquaint them, first, with the shape and sounds of letters, then with simple words, eventually with suitable books.

Moreover, with children, we encourage. We praise small gains. We're patient—not perfectionists. When setbacks or errors occur, we do *not* scold, harangue, tyrannize, or warn of bad things to come.

For ourselves, now we ask: "What or who thwarted me when I was young?" We could correct

---

53. 1 Corinthians 6:19-29; 2 Corinthians 6:16

erroneous lessons by observing those who seem the very opposite of anyone from whom we learned to be afraid. Timing counts. We may want to do this precisely when we are most fearful, not just when everything's rosy.

With "simple trust" the goal is to *internalize* calm reassurance, exactly when we're terrified of losing a job, money, friends, our spouse, our health. To ourselves, we'll sound "like a mother hen who gathereth her chicks under her wings."

In this case, I mean to say you *can* be your own loving, wholesome mother. And you *are* your own vulnerable little chick.

These ideas are not about changing situations—although that could and regularly does occur.

Our "gentle mother tone" can help us trust in God and "lean not unto our own understanding."[54]

My secular friends might scoff at the notion of God's love, or at the concept of "simple trust." Nevertheless, my track record with this sort of re-education is solid.

---

54. Proverbs 3:5

For decades, I've helped my ultra-successful, competitive clients in such areas of development. One need not use theological terms to convey *spiritual* notions.

Almost everyone, the world over, is spiritual in the healthy sense implied here.

It's also obvious that some who talk in the most pious way can house the most rigid, vengeful, unholy hearts.

Poet and author Rainer Maria Rilke framed these thoughts in universal, not exactly biblical, terms.

Thus in summary, and the wish that your days might be bountifully full of peace and true joy, I offer these lines to you:

> *Perhaps everything dangerous and frightening is something helpless that just wants help from us.*[55]

෨

---

55. R.M Rilke, Franz X. Kapus. *Letters to a Young Poet,* 1954 revised ed., New York. Norton Books. (Paraphrased)

ACKNOWLEDGEMENTS

Thank you to Mary Mobert, my friend, near-by neighbor, and editor in her own right, for proofreading the manuscript during various phases of production. Thank you to Fred Andrle, poet, award-winning radio host, and long time friend, for proofing the last iteration of this book just prior to printing.

I am grateful for their help. All remaining errors are my own.

ABOUT THE AUTHOR

After a notable career in public education, Marsha Sinetar founded her solo practice of leadership development for the private sector. And began to write. Her outlook transcends age, culture, or occupation, as evidenced by her professional reach and broad range of ideas and authorship.

Since the 1980s, the prolific Sinetar has received acclaim from such groups as *Body, Mind, Spirit Magazine*, the *Athena Mentoring and Publishing Award*, *Catholic Press Association Award* for a self-illustrated children's book, and last year, the *Folio Digital Magazine* prize for article excellence.

The Christian contemplative continues to develop leadership talent through her dialogue sessions, living and working at home, "as simply and quietly as possible."

For more information, please visit www.marshasinetar.com.

Notes and Thoughts

Notes and Thoughts

Notes and Thoughts

Notes and Thoughts

Notes and Thoughts

Notes and Thoughts

Notes and Thoughts

"He said unto them, Go ye into all the world, and preach the gospel to every creature."

Mark 16:15

Made in United States
Orlando, FL
15 June 2023

34162314R00069